Shapes: Rectangles

Esther Sarfatti

ROURKE PUBLISHING

www.rourkepublishing.com

www.rourkepublishing.com

PHOTO CREDITS: © Nicole S. Young: title page; © Dragan Trifunovic: page 5; © Viorika Prikhodko: page 7; © Renee Brady: page 9; © Jody Dingle: page 11; © Graeme Mowday: page 13; © Bonita Hein: page 15; © Jeroen Peys: page 17; © Eva Serrabassa: page 19; © Marzanna Syncerz: page 21; © Vladimir Kondrachov: page 23.

Editor: Robert Stengard-Olliges

Cover design by Nicola Stratford.

Library of Congress Cataloging-in-Publication Data

Sarfatti, Esther.
  Shapes : rectangles / Esther Sarfatti.
    p. cm. -- (Concepts)
  ISBN 978-1-60044-526-2 (Hardcover)
  ISBN 978-1-60044-667-2 (Softcover)
  1. Rectangles--Juvenile literature. 2. Shapes--Juvenile literature. I. Title.
    QA484.S268 2008
    516'.154--dc22
                          2007014074

Rourke Publishing
Printed in the United States of America, North Mankato, Minnesota
030411
030411LP-B

www.rourkepublishing.com - rourke@rourkepublishing.com
Post Office Box 643328 Vero Beach, Florida 32964

This is a rectangle.

Rectangles are everywhere.

Books are rectangles.

7

This door is a rectangle.

This wagon is a rectangle.

This swimming pool is a rectangle.

This bed is a rectangle.

15

This game has rectangles.

These presents are rectangles.

19

This sandbox is a rectangle.

21

Rectangles are everywhere. Can you find the rectangles?

23

Index

Further Reading

Leake, Diyan. *Finding Shapes: Rectangles*. Heinemann, 2005.

Olson, Nathan. *Rectangles Around Town*. A+ Books, 2007.

Recommended Websites

www.enchantedlearning.com/themes/shapes.shtml

About the Author

Esther Sarfatti has worked with children's books for over 15 years as an editor and translator. This is her first series as an author. Born in Brooklyn, New York, and brought up in a trilingual home, Esther currently lives with her husband and son in Madrid, Spain.